D1717139

SCHOLASTIC
News
Nonfiction Readers

Dinosaur Eggs

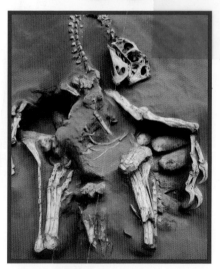

by Susan H. Gray

Children's Press®
A Division of Scholastic Inc.
New York Toronto London Auckland Sydney
Mexico City New Delhi Hong Kong
Danbury, Connecticut

These content vocabulary word builders are for grades 1–2.

Subject Consultant: Rudyard W. Sadleir, Doctoral Candidate in Evolutionary Biology, University of Chicago, Chicago, Illinois

Reading Consultant: Cecilia Minden-Cupp, PhD, Former Director of the Language and Literacy Program, Harvard Graduate School of Education, Cambridge, Massachusetts

Photographs © 2007: AP/Wide World Photos/David A. Sommers/The Saginaw News: 15 bottom; Corbis images: 20 top (Ron Austing/Frank Lane Picture Agency), 7 inset (Bettmann), 21 bottom (Gary W. Carter), 4 bottom left, 6 (David Muench), 23 (Robert Pickett), cover, 2, 5 top right, 13 (University of the Witwatersrand/epa); Natural History Museum, London: 19 (John Sibbick), 4 bottom right, 12; Photo Researchers, NY: 5 bottom left, 9 (E. R. Degginger), 21 top (Sinclair Stammers); Science Faction Images/ Louie Psihoyos: back cover, 1, 4 top, 5 bottom right, 11, 15 top, 17, 20 bottom; The Image Works/Topham: 5 top left, 7.

Book Design: Simonsays Design!
Book Production: The Design Lab

Library of Congress Cataloging-in-Publication Data
Gray, Susan Heinrichs.
    Dinosaur eggs / by Susan H. Gray.
        p. cm. — (Scholastic news nonfiction readers)
    Includes bibliographical references and index.
    ISBN-13: 978-0-531-17483-8
    ISBN-10: 0-531-17483-2
    1. Dinosaurs—Eggs—Juvenile literature. 2. Fossils—Juvenile literature.
    I. Title. II. Series.
    QE861.6.E35G73 2007
    567.9—dc22   2006024046

1 2 3 4 5 6 7 8 9 10 R 16 15 14 13 12 11 10 09 08 07

CONTENTS

WORD HUNT

Look for these words as you read. They will be in **bold**.

acid
(**ass**-id)

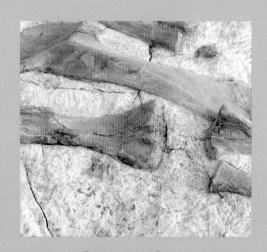

fossils
(**foss**-uhlz)

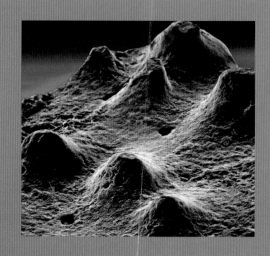

pores
(porz)

4

desert
(**dehz**-urt)

embryo
(**em**-bree-oh)

reptiles
(**rep**-tylz)

skeletons
(**skell**-uh-tuhnz)

5

A GREAT FIND

In 1923, a man named Roy Chapman Andrews found potato-shaped egg **fossils** in the **desert**. Fossils are the remains of plants and animals that lived millions of years ago.

fossils

Roy Chapman Andrews found dinosaur egg fossils at this spot in the Gobi Desert.

Roy Chapman Andrews knew that the egg fossils came from a dinosaur.

The fossil eggs made news all over the world. But no one should have been surprised.

Dinosaurs were **reptiles**. And reptiles are animals that lay eggs. So of course, dinosaurs laid eggs!

An iguana rests next to her eggs. Like
iguanas, dinosaurs were reptiles.

Fossils of dinosaur eggs and nests have been found at about two hundred places around the world.

Some fossil eggs are round, and some are long. Some are as small as bird eggs. Others are almost the size of footballs!

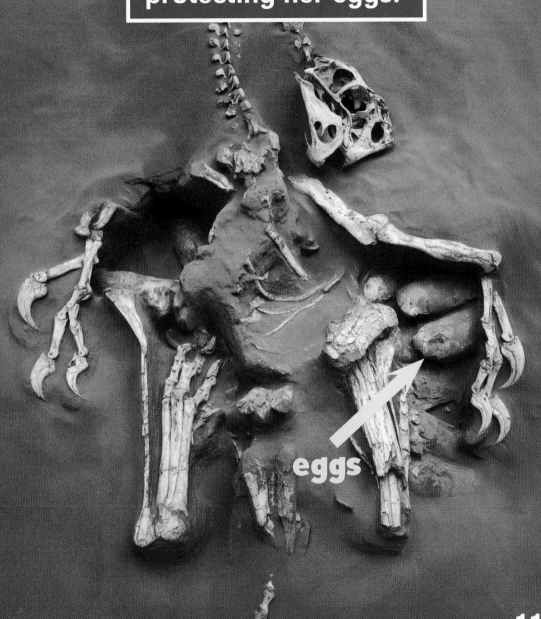

This *Oviraptor* died protecting her eggs.

eggs

Dinosaur eggshells are covered with tiny holes called **pores**. These little holes let air in and out. The developing baby dinosaur, or **embryo**, growing inside needed the air.

pores

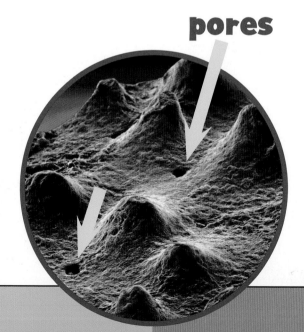

The bones of a dinosaur embryo were discovered inside this fossil egg.

There are different ways to see the embryo inside a fossil egg.

You might use **acid** to eat away the rock surrounding the embryo. This can take months.

A special machine can also be used to see inside a fossil egg. This takes just minutes.

A scientist soaks fossil eggs in acid.

A scientist places a fossil egg in a machine that will show him what is inside.

15

Many fossil eggs are cracked and empty. But others have little dinosaur **skeletons** inside.

The tiny dinosaurs had big heads. They also had arms, legs, and tails. Some even had little claws.

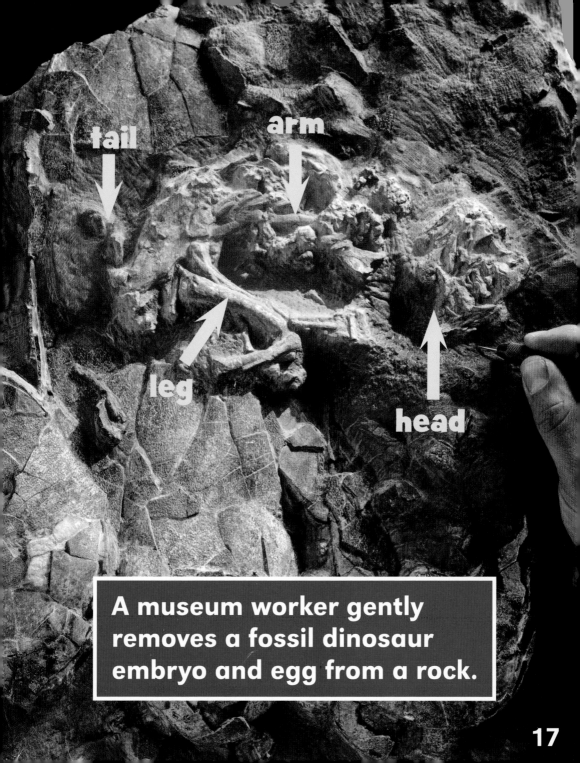

tail

arm

leg

head

A museum worker gently removes a fossil dinosaur embryo and egg from a rock.

People have found dinosaur nests with only a few eggs. They have also found nests with more than twenty eggs!

Maybe some baby dinosaurs grew up in big families. Maybe others had to grow up on their own. Scientists don't know for sure. What do you think?

Maiasaura mothers laid their eggs at nesting sites. Scientists think they took care of their babies.

WHAT DO EGGS TELL US?

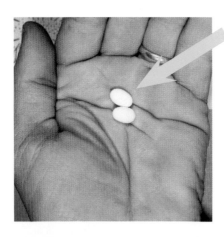

Hummingbird Eggs
Tiny eggs come from very small animals.

Dinosaur Egg Fossil
Large eggs come from large animals.

Dinosaur Fossil Egg Nest

Round eggs were probably laid in a nest. If they were laid on the ground, they might roll away!

Speckled Bird Eggs

Speckled eggs are often laid out in the open. Their markings help them blend in with their surroundings.

YOUR NEW WORDS

acid (**ass**-id) a chemical that can dissolve things

desert (**dehz**-urt) a dry area that gets very little rain

embryo (**em**-bree-oh) a developing animal that is not yet hatched

fossils (**foss**-uhlz) remains of plants or animals from millions of years ago

pores (porz) tiny holes

reptiles (**rep**-tylz) scaly animals that usually lay eggs

skeletons (**skell**-uh-tuhnz) the entire sets of the bones of animals

HOW DOES AN EMBRYO GROW?

Day One

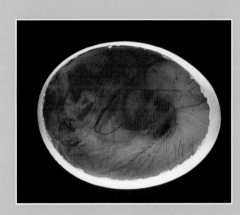

Day Ten

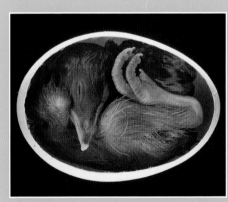

Day Twenty-One

Hatched!

INDEX

FIND OUT MORE

Book:

Dussling, Jennifer. *Dinosaur Eggs*. New York: Grosset & Dunlap, 2000.

Website:

ZoomDinosaurs.com
www.enchantedlearning.com/subjects/dinosaurs

MEET THE AUTHOR

Susan H. Gray has a master's degree in zoology. She has written more than seventy science and reference books for children. She especially loves to write about animals. Susan and her husband, Michael, live in Cabot, Arkansas.